T0414371

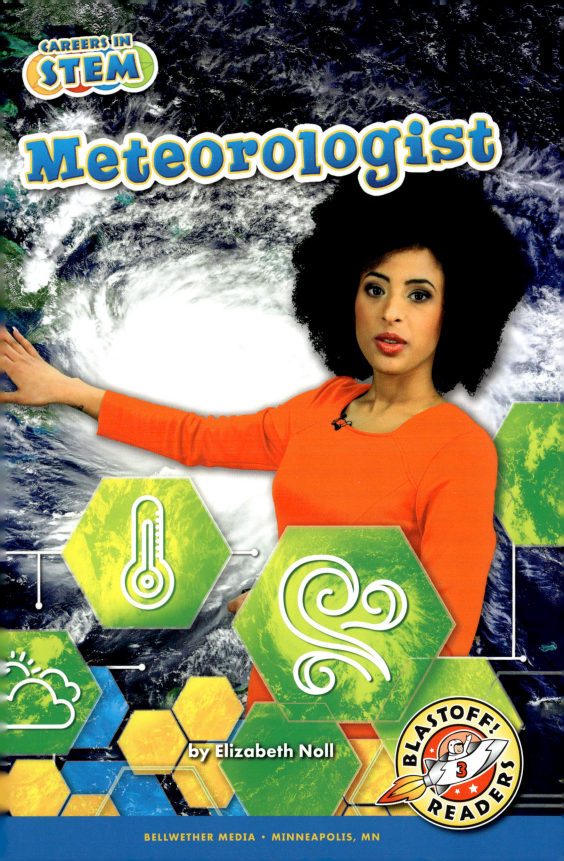

Meteorologist

by Elizabeth Noll

BLASTOFF!
3
READERS

BELLWETHER MEDIA • MINNEAPOLIS, MN

Blastoff! Readers are carefully developed by literacy experts to build reading stamina and move students toward fluency by combining standards-based content with developmentally appropriate text.

Level 1 provides the most support through repetition of high-frequency words, light text, predictable sentence patterns, and strong visual support.

Level 2 offers early readers a bit more challenge through varied sentences, increased text load, and text-supportive special features.

Level 3 advances early-fluent readers toward fluency through increased text load, less reliance on photos, advancing concepts, longer sentences, and more complex special features.

★ **Blastoff! Universe**

Reading Level

Grade **K**

Grades **1–3**

Grade **4**

This edition first published in 2023 by Bellwether Media, Inc.

No part of this publication may be reproduced in whole or in part without written permission of the publisher. For information regarding permission, write to Bellwether Media, Inc., Attention: Permissions Department, 6012 Blue Circle Drive, Minnetonka, MN 55343.

Library of Congress Cataloging-in-Publication Data

LC record for Meteorologist available at: https://lccn.loc.gov/2022005468

Text copyright © 2023 by Bellwether Media, Inc. BLASTOFF! READERS and associated logos are trademarks and/or registered trademarks of Bellwether Media, Inc.

Editor: Betsy Rathburn   Designer: Andrea Schneider

Printed in the United States of America, North Mankato, MN.

Table of **Contents**

Storm Warning

The snowstorm is coming fast. It brings strong wind and a lot of snow.

The family turns on the TV. A meteorologist warns them to be careful. There could be a **blizzard**!

blizzard

What Is a Meteorologist?

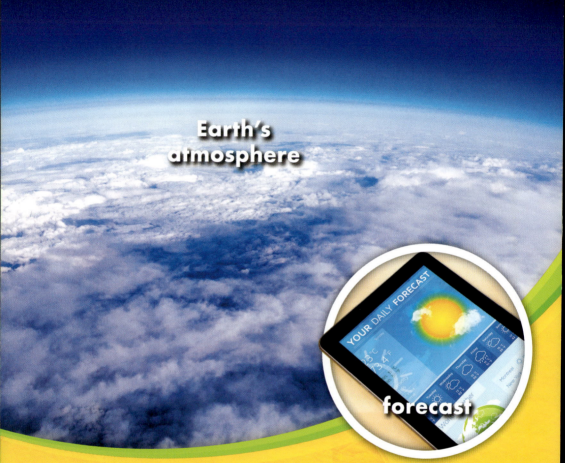

Earth's
atmosphere

forecast

Meteorologists are scientists.
They study the weather.

They look at what is happening in the **atmosphere**. They make **forecasts**. They look at how weather changes from day to day.

Famous Meteorologist

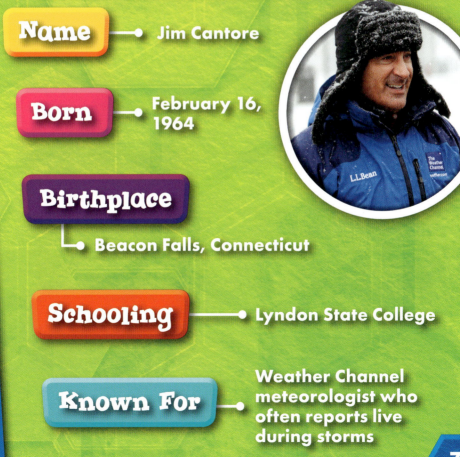

Name → Jim Cantore

Born → February 16, 1964

Birthplace → Beacon Falls, Connecticut

Schooling → Lyndon State College

Known For → Weather Channel meteorologist who often reports live during storms

Meteorologists work in many places. Some do **research** at schools. Others work for the government.

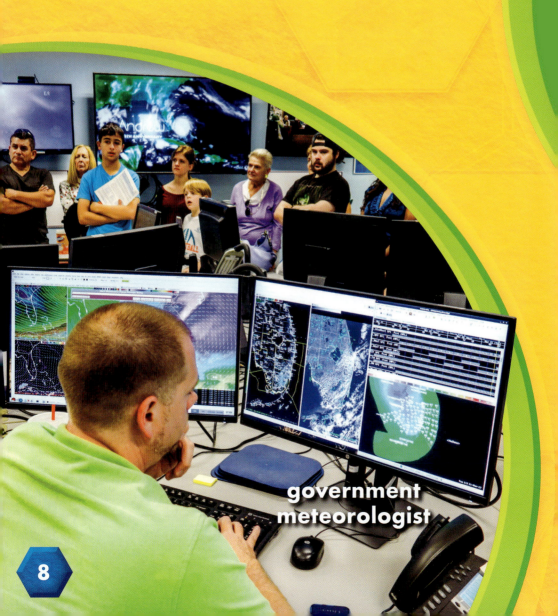

government meteorologist

TV meteorologist

Some work on TV. Their forecasts
tell what the weather will be like.

Meteorologists measure wind and heat. They also measure **humidity** and **air pressure**.

They **compare** it to past **data**. They use computer **models** to help. This helps them make **predictions**.

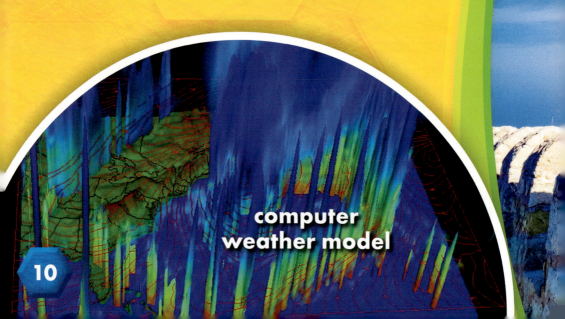

computer weather model

tool used
to measure
wind speed

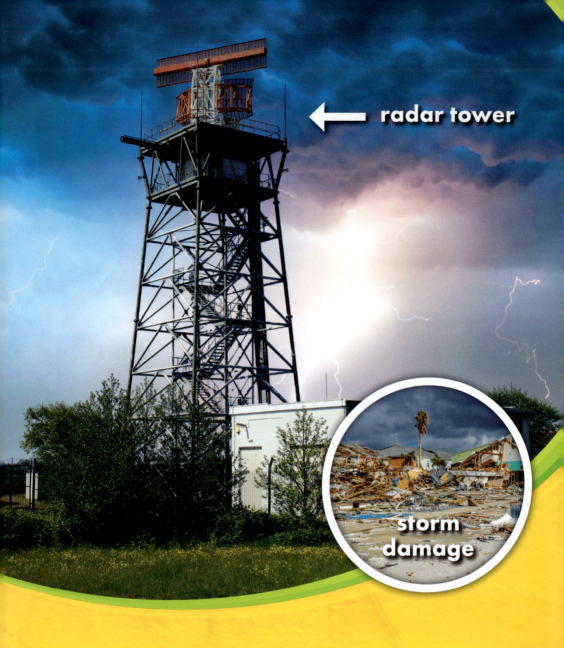

radar tower

storm damage

Radar helps track weather as it moves. Meteorologists look for signs that a storm could cause damage.

They warn people who live in its path. They share what to expect and how to keep safe.

Meteorology in Real Life

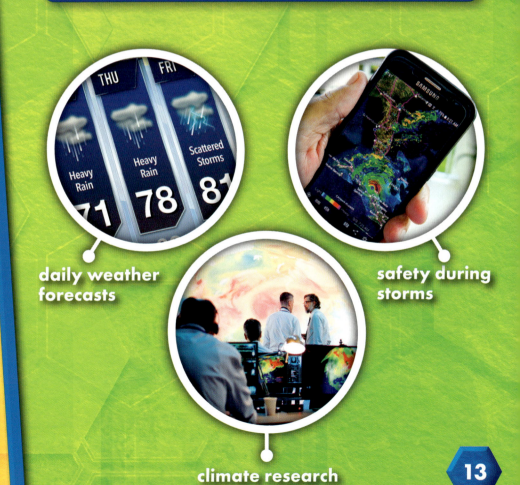

daily weather forecasts

safety during storms

climate research

Some meteorologists study **climate change**. They look at past data. They study how it has changed over time.

Using STEM

Science — test ideas about the weather

Technology — use computers to study weather data

Engineering — design ways to measure the weather

Math — predict where storms will go

This helps them understand what future weather might be like.

Becoming a Meteorologist

Meteorologists like to research.
They are also good with computers.

16

Most study science in college. They take classes in math. They also learn about **physics** and **chemistry**.

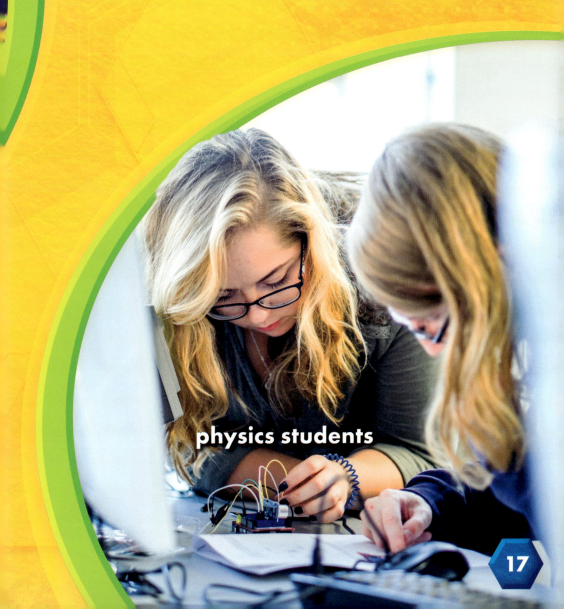

physics students

Many meteorologists go to **graduate school**. They choose a weather topic to study further.

They research the topic. They present their work. They become **experts**!

Then, they get jobs. Some work for companies that forecast weather. Others do research. Some teach students how to study weather.

How to Become a Meteorologist

1 study meteorology in college

2 continue studying in graduate school

3 find a job at a company, school, or government group

Meteorologists have important jobs. They help people stay safe in all weather!

Glossary

air pressure—the force of air pressing down on things

atmosphere—the mixture of gases that surround the earth

blizzard—a severe snowstorm with strong winds

chemistry—a science that deals with substances and the changes they go through

climate change—a human-caused change in Earth's weather due to warming temperatures

compare—to note how alike or different things are

data—information

experts—people who have a lot of knowledge or experience in a certain area

forecasts—predictions of future weather based on data collected

graduate school—a school where people study a specialty area after college

humidity—a measure of how much water is in the air

models—systems or processes that help scientists make predictions

physics—a science that deals with matter, energy, heat, light, electricity, motion, and sound

predictions—guesses about future events

radar—a tool used to track storms

research—careful study to find new knowledge or information about something

To Learn More

AT THE LIBRARY

Kerry, Isaac. *Climate Change and Extreme Weather.* Minneapolis, Minn.: Lerner Publications, 2023.

Noll, Elizabeth. *Climate Scientist.* Minneapolis, Minn.: Bellwether Media, 2023.

Stoller-Conrad, Jessica. *Weather Experiments Book for Kids: More Than 25 Hands-On Activities to Learn About Rain, Wind, Hurricanes, and More.* Emeryville, Calif.: Rockridge Press, 2021.

ON THE WEB

FACTSURFER

Factsurfer.com gives you a safe, fun way to find more information.

1. Go to www.factsurfer.com.

2. Enter "meteorologist" into the search box and click 🔍.

3. Select your book cover to see a list of related content.

Index

The images in this book are reproduced through the courtesy of: tomazl, front cover (meteorologist); Evgeniyqw, front cover (background); LilKar, p. 3; lpedan, p. 4 (blizzard); Africa Studio, pp. 4-5; leeborn, pp. 6-7; ra2 studio, p. 6 (forecast); The Editorialist/ Alamy, p. 7 (Jim Cantore); Jeffrey Isaac Greenberg 14+/ Alamy, p. 8; Andrey Burmakin, pp. 8-9; H.S. Photos/ Alamy, p. 10 (computer weather model); Artem Kontratiev, pp. 10-11; Barrie Harwood/ Alamy, pp. 12-13; Terry Kelly, p. 12 (storm damage); SpiffyJ, p. 13 (daily weather forecasts); imac/ Alamy, p. 13 (safety during storms); Frame Stock Footage, p. 13 (climate research); David R. Frazier Photolibrary, Inc./ Alamy, pp. 14-15; Leo Morgan, pp. 16-17; aberCPC/ Alamy, p. 17; Jeffrey Isaac Greenberg 12+/ Alamy, p. 18 (inset); Photoagriculture, pp. 18-19; Thomas Andreas, pp. 20-21 (meteorologist); Fine Arts/ Alamy, pp. 20-21 (top); vitaliy_73, p. 23 (hat); Alexeysun, p. 23 (umbrella).